What is it like to ride into space?
Meet some men and women who
will become astronauts.

We have to learn a lot about the spacecraft.

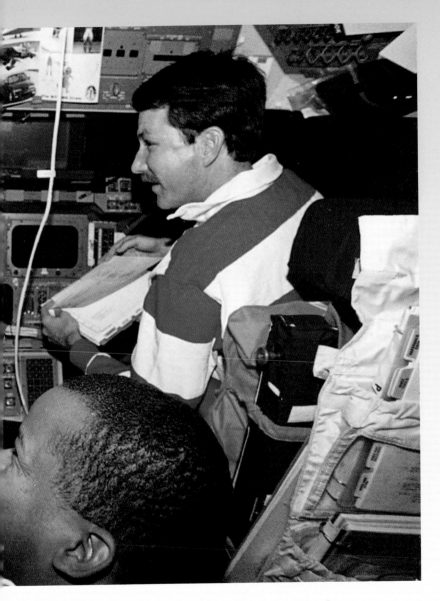

We must know how to make
everything work.

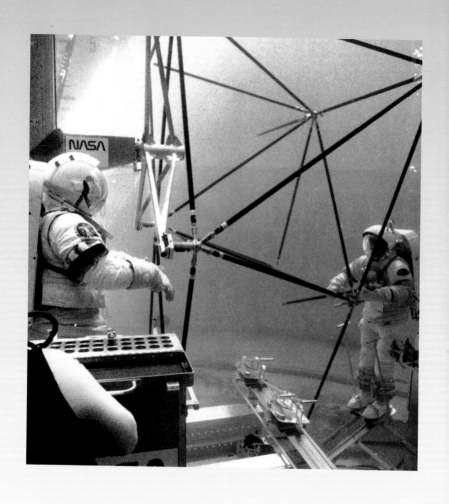

We might have to fix something
outside the spacecraft. We
practice in a pool. In space, we
will float like this, too.

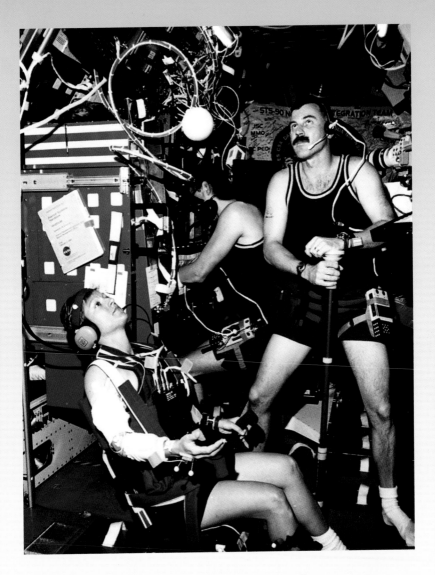

Machines help us to work out in space. We need to stay strong and healthy.

A spacecraft may land in the wrong place.

So we learn to take care of
ourselves.

We do not mind the hard work.
Going into space is a dream
come true.